There Are Four Trees On Your Stone

There Are Four Trees On Your Stone

Jean Leonard

Copyright © 2013 by Jean Leonard.

ISBN: Softcover   978-1-4797-9545-1
          Ebook   978-1-4797-9546-8

All rights reserved. No part of this book may be reproduced or transmitted in any form or by any means, electronic or mechanical, including photocopying, recording, or by any information storage and retrieval system, without permission in writing from the copyright owner.

This book was printed in the United States of America.

Rev. date: 02/14/2013

To order additional copies of this book, contact:
Xlibris Corporation
1-888-795-4274
www.Xlibris.com
Orders@Xlibris.com
130577

Introduction

When you are a 28-year-old white woman reporter, with a newspaper editor husband and a college administrator father, and you find a stone on a holy Lakota mountain, and a Lakota holy man says, "Do you see the four trees on this stone?" you look and see only four fern leaves fossilized on the stone. When he says "You will meet four men in 9,2,4, and 8" and points to some fossilized numbers in the corner of the stone, you are skeptical and offer to give him the stone.

When he says, "No, it is your stone," you do keep it. And over the next two years, when in September, February, April, and August, you meet four men of the bloodlines of great Lakota (Sioux) and Apache, you start honoring the stone, and the mountain you found it on. You start paying close attention to the holy man, Frank Fools Crow, and his wife Kate, who is the mother you never had.

This book is the story of finding the four men, the four trees. It is the story of what they and Fools Crow taught me as we traveled several states together. There were powerful adventures at North and South Dakota and Montana reservations and universities, a Minnesota sacred pipestone quarry and Minnesota maximum security prison, a California publishing company, and Alaska cities. These are places where September, February, April, and August brought four holy men.

The skeptical "just the facts, man" white woman began to see the connectedness of all of life. On Bear Butte near Sturgis, South Dakota, where Crazy Horse had fasted, she gave her life to the Great Spirit, because her energies were being miserably unused and the world was going by without her doing something she felt she should be doing.

In exchange for her offering up her life, the stone glowed, a tree gave a loving message, stars fell, and she would never feel alone again.

I am writing this, my story, so that these people can live on.

Dedicated to the four trees, women teachers, and Kate and Frank Fools Crow

Tree One
Eagle Man*

In 1968, at 28, I went to Sturgis, South Dakota, and climbed Crazy Horse's Bear Butte vision hill. I found a stone and took it to the wise Fools Crow, holy man and acknowledged leader on the Pine Ridge (S.D.) reservation until his death in 1989. "In September, February, April, and August, you will meet four trees." He'd seen the 9-2-4-8 and four trees fossilized onto the stone.

That August, I had already met the first tree on the stone. Eagle Man was a decorated Lakota pilot and law student who led me to Fools Crow, a Sun Dance, and Bear Butte. He would also have a part in my meeting each of the other three trees.

The next chapters will tell of Fools Crow's ceremony to protect Eagle Man in Vietnam. His phantom jet came through heavy flak in 110 missions.

*Credits for photos are on the last page of the book.

Tree Two
Long Elk

In September 1968, the first tree, Eagle Man, told me of the second tree. In December, in Vermillion, South Dakota, at the University of South Dakota, he introduced me to Long Elk. In February, the Bear Butte stone glowed in his hands, then other sacred events and prophecies of leaders to come unfolded with this second decorated Lakota pilot. Long Elk told me that my love for his people made his own load easier to bear. And I knew my own past made my new path necessary. The harmony and sacred healing traditions were that much more important to one with a mentally ill mother.

The amazing experiences with this man who had survived three plane crashes and was declared dead during service in three wars, are in the following chapters.

His 18 months in a Korean prisoner of war camp could not defeat him. He used his grandfather's training there as he had in World War II when he evaded capture in Japan.

Tree Three
Red Horse's Fire

In June, 1969, I went up Bear Butte again, this time with the sacred holy man, Fools Crow. I later went to California to work for a publisher Fools Crow also had taken on this second vision quest. As I drove into the parking lot, that publisher met me at the car and gave me the job of editing and adding to his book on Crazy Horse. The editor had just called and resigned due to illness. I was used to these "coincidences" by then.

Soon after arriving at that publishing company in California, I met the third Lakota tree Fools Crow had seen on the stone. An ex-paratrooper and now author, Red Horse's Fire was working on his book about the coming of the dawn for Native America. The book was tied to Mexico. We arrived at the sacred, world's oldest living tree in El Tule, Oaxaca (wa-ha-ca), Mexico on the most sacred Zapotec day, February second. I remembered the 9-2(February)-4-8 prophecy. The seed of the tree was being blessed as for thousands of years. Bands were playing; the Zapoteca (People of the Clouds) were honoring ancient traditions and beliefs.

We completed work on his book, based on the Aztec calendar, prophesying that the dawn would break, returning mankind's respect for earth. This would put a bright glow back into her, our earth mother.

I was beginning to understand I could use the Lakota harmony with each other, self, earth, and creator to heal my mentally ill birth mother, as the Lakota were using them to cure their earth mother. Soon Mother was in Kansas blossoming under the sunlight of the great Karl Menninger, and my new Lakota insights.

Tree and the Church

An ancient church now stands in the shadow of the "*Tree*" recalling its sacredness.

Tree with Children

Part of the trunk of the "*Zapotec Tree of Life*," El Tule, Oaxaca in Mexico.

Tree Four
Wolf of Yukon

Soon the third tree was out of my life. The sacred ceremonies and events happening still with the first and second trees were leading me into the spirit world. These events and powerful people, I describe in the following chapters.

In a Minnesota prison in August, 1972, the fourth tree (an Apache-Lakota Marine pilot and graduate physicist) saw me dressed in black, white, red, and yellow (honoring the four winds and four races). He approached me and said he had been told I was coming. In nearly a year of visiting him at the prison (while I wrote for the St. Paul Public Schools Indian Ed. Dept.) he spoke of his beautiful Yukon and Alaska country. His ancestors, Chiracahua Apache (southern Athabascans) and Lakota (Sioux) had gone to the Yukon when the killing started and settled with northern Athabascans.

In 1975, we met again in Fairbanks, Alaska, and though he soon was gone, for nearly 25 years I worked in Alaska among his Athabascan people and with the Eskimo people and fell in love with the earth mother as she is when undisturbed by advancing populations.

With just a correspondence education from Juneau, Alaska, Wolf of Yukon had been given a scholarship to the Massachusetts Institute of Technology in Boston. In his late teens he left the pristine forests of rural Yukon Territory wilderness for urban Boston. He would be very lonely and overwhelmed with the crowded conditions. He would look out his window and see this statue (Henry Moore's model for his larger one at Lincoln Center, New York City). The homesick, lonely Wolf of Yukon would go and sit on its lap and let the snow fall on him, or study there.

When he told me this, I hoped to see that statue one day. Forty years later, in 2012, I did, and sat on its lap. I have no photo of Wolf of Yukon.

During the Holy Months Women Also Were Sent to Me

Native American women also were to cross my path during the years after I found the stone. Ignatia Broker, an Ojibway elder, and I had a long friendship in Minneapolis-St. Paul in the 1970s after meeting while working at an Indian organization. One day she told her grandmother's story. The government had said the Ojibway must go to the reservation when the snow stopped. So that year the snows didn't stop until summer. The forests did not want to give up their people. I said "If you'll speak your grandmother's life into a tape recorder, I'll type it into chapters." So she did. We wanted to call it *The Forest Cried* but the Minnesota State Historical Society called it *Night Flying Woman* after the grandmother's ability to dream significant dreams. It won Ignatia the Woman of the Year award at a ceremony in New York City. She had wanted to dedicate the book to me, but I said that would make only one person happy. She could dedicate it to her people and make more people happy. At that time the traditional Ojibway were in conflict with the militant Ojibway. So Ignatia dedicated the book to both these groups who were working for their people. She used the dedication to bring them together.

In Fairbanks, Alaska, I met Emily Brown in U. of Alaska native languages classes. This Inupiaq (Eskimo) elder took me to her Bering Sea home where the local lady "chief" told this story. The government people wanted to divide up the land to individual people. The officials were told it was a matter of summer and winter camps the people needed to move between. When taken to the summer camps and there was no trash or dirty diapers, the officials didn't believe the camps had been used! Emily was a beloved dignitary at the U. of Alaska. When Washington, D.C., officials came, Emily was asked to welcome them. This tiny little lady would go up and rub noses with them. "We were told that is how Eskimos kiss," she would say, smiling. She also taped and I transcribed a book on her experiences as a youth being sent to a far away boarding school and other life stories. I never knew if it was published. As a reward for this work, she flew me to her Bering Sea home at Unalakleet. Berry picking with Emily in the Fairbanks area was great. She knew the good spots and taught me to pick up any berries I spilled. During long winters, her people had saved food with a passion, because it had to last until spring.

In Memory

This book is a love letter to all the Lakota and others who did not know Frank and Kate Fools Crow. This great holy man and his wife healed, cheered, and gave hope to a people who had been hurt deeply. Parting clouds and healing people who had been called incurable was just part of the power Frank had. Kate was a mother to them all. In their three room cabin, and on trips in my VW bug, they showed a searching 28-year-old woman what it is to be a loving, caring husband and grandfather, wife and grandmother. In their near century of life, they brought their people through culture shock and saved the ceremonies from government and religious annihilation. Their belief system can teach a hurting world harmony with earth, each other, self, and creator. I pray their power flows through my words into you.

Chapter One

When the Volkswagen first pulled onto the Fools Crow ranch, Frank Fools Crow's grandson was standing in the front yard. Kyle, South Dakota, had not been hard to find, and the directions to his ranch had not been complicated. What the nine-year old thought when the funny looking "bug" pulled up and a sun-burned, freckled 28-year old white lady emerged can only be imagined.

I had seen him a week earlier helping Fools Crow as the holy man conducted the August, 1968, Sun Dance in Pine Ridge, S.D. Tall and majestic does not describe adequately this holy man in his ceremonial robe and sacred symbols. His other name is Bear Eagle. When his sharp, eagle eyes looked into your soul, you knew his eyes saw you way deeply.

The boy took me to see Fool Crow in the three room cabin on the ranch. I handed him the stone I had found on Bear Butte (Crazy Horse's fasting place) the previous day. After having fasted many hours, I had looked down at my car and thought "I can never make it back down there." Instantly, there came some power and I nearly flew down. The same energy propelled me to his ranch.

The great man, dressed now in western shirt and slacks, not looking his 70-some years, took the stone. He introduced me to his wife, Kate, and we sat and talked. Kate's warmth and acceptance reached out loudly without a word. I showed them the sacred pipe bowl carved from a Minnesota pipestone quarry block of the sacred stone by my former husband. Though a white man, he had known I should have it on Bear Butte, and would want to offer it to Fools Crow.

Somehow, before I left the Fools Crows' cabin, it was accepted that I would return home, get a tent, and come camp with them the rest of the summer. As I was getting ready to leave, Frank gave me back the stone. "You will meet four trees in 9, 2, 4 and 8."

I looked at the stone and saw the four fossilized fern leaves that could be taken as trees and saw where he pointed to the 9-2-4 and 8. He was being guided now, I know, by his spirit guides to read all this. But at the time I was a typical white daughter of a college instructor and former wife of a newspaper editor. I saw only the fossilized images on the stone. "If you want, keep it," I said. "No. It is your stone."

I had no idea then how powerful that stone was, how it would react to people I would meet, and how many nights I would get through by holding it close to me and sleeping with it under my pillow.

After gathering my tent and a few belongings into the VW at my former home in eastern South Dakota, where I put out the "Great Plains Observer." I again crossed South Dakota to the holy couple's ranch. The first night was very lonely, then I heard a sweet, young musical voice "Grandpa say house too crowded. I stay here with you." It was Billy Pawnee Leggins, their nine-year-old adopted grandson, who had been in the Sun Dance, a most dignified and endearing youngster with a black robe tied around his waist during the dance, eyes closed, lips tight, praying deeply. He had danced next to the pilot who had returned from Vietnam fulfilling an earlier prophecy he would dance in the Sun Dance with a young Lakota.

When Eagle Man had been Billy's age, he was living near the Pine Ridge Reservation badlands, which the military had used for bombing practice during World War II. When he was school age, his mother hid him when the Catholic schools sent people to pick up children So he grew up knowing the Lakota holy ways.

Before he was shipped out with the Marines to Vietnam, Fools Crow held a Yuipi ceremony for him to protect him. When told he would be protected, he vowed that on his return he would dance in the Sun Dance. In 110 missions flying through heavy flak his phantom jet was protected. So when he returned, he danced in the Sun Dance for several years.

During this time, he attended the University of South Dakota and received a law degree. His articles in my "Great Plains Observer" opened his mind to the idea "the pen is mightier than the sword." After years in law and in airport management, he would become the author of many books and owner of Four Directions Publishing in Minnesota.

And he was a hero to Pine Ridge Reservation youth including Billy, who danced beside him in that sun dance where I first saw Billy and Fools Crow. I had met Eagle Man at an Indian Mystique Seminar. When I showed him a copy of my magazine he suggested

I attend an upcoming Sun Dance where I saw the Fools Crows. It was an honor that when they saw me drive up that day they looked deep, not just at my color.

To understand Frank and Kate, you will be helped by the story of how they adopted Billy. He was born along a blacktop road, and taken to Frank and Kate, though they were nearing their 70's. Told of where he had been born, they named him Chunku (road—which with sapa or black added means black road). Anyway, he, like many Native Americans was allergic to milk. So they gave him coffee and healing things from the earth and welcomed the tiny infant to their hearts.

How much bravery it took the nine-year-old to go to the strange lady's tent, I've often marveled at. But my husband's name had been Bill and I smiled at the powers that be over the friendly gesture of sending another Billy to ease my loneliness. We roamed the woods and creek together and he slowly taught me some Lakota words and told me about the little people to be seen along the creek sometimes.

Invited to my first powwow on the Rosebud Reservation, one feels quite humble and grateful. We camped together, the old holy ones, their grandchildren, and a wide-eyed white lady.

Driving to a healing ceremony in Lame Deer, Montana, Frank was in the front seat of the VW, Kate and Billy in the back. Such joy and laughs I heard on that trip as they noticed all the little four-leggeds out the window I hadn't been raised to notice. The tradition was to pull up to the house of the person one was to heal and wait in the car until they noticed. Then they would come out and invite us in.

I was so impressed by Frank that evening as he used his roots from the Earth Mother and a warm lubricant to heal the person. As we were driving, sometimes he would have me stop and he would get a plant he had remembered was there.

Then it came time for me to go to a job at the University of South Dakota Indian Ed. Dept., and for Billy to be taken (not willingly) to a Catholic boarding school. I was so afraid they would try to take away his sacred Lakota ways, I wrote the following for my magazine.

Letter to a mission school:

You have a precious property in one of those third floor rows of bunks.

He had one little suitcase when our Volkswagen pulled away from the reservation ranch he had roamed ever since soon after his birth. His two "old folks" (as he called them in loneliness one night when they'd gone on to a powwow and we were to join them the next day) directed my hesitations at the crossroads. And, with the little English they knew, covering up for my utter ignorance of their lovely Lakota, they also directed my stops at the corner trading posts. New school shoes we never found, so the tennis shoes would have to serve, tied or untied, as fate willed.

New underwear was found, however, and forced by big sister, onto a reluctant back seat victim. Sunflower seeds in one hand and popsicle in the other, eased the pain somewhat.

Please, mission school, don't change this boy. Don't convert him.

He doesn't know what baptism is. If you ask him about communion, his face will be blank.

But this boy has a holy, wise spirit far beyond his eight years.

You'll see him stand sometimes, his eyes closed and his lips tight. He is praying.

He'll roam off into the woods back of the mission sometimes, all by himself. Please don't disturb him. He's going to his sanctuary.

He may not tell you—he would scarcely mention it to me as we roamed the hills and he camped out with me back of his "old folks"—that those birds most of us have never gotten inside of and flown around in, have a song they sing—just to him.

He won't rebel probably. He'll be obedient.

The old man who has been his father-grandfather is a Lakota holy man. He is kind, he is firm in his sense of right. This boy feels deeply the meaning of the genuinely religious ceremonies the holy man conducts. And the boy's joy is deep and pure when he is asked to have a part in these ceremonies.

Please mission school, don't make religion complicated for this boy. Don't teach him he as to go through people or actions to be with his friend, Wakan Tanka, (Great Spirit) his Father Sky, or his Mother Earth.

That communion has been there for a long time. There need be no other.

And please mission school, don't encrust his outlook on life with pious words and complicated rules. Let him continue the same sense he has of simple dedication to the will of that to which the boy prays.

If his attention is kept on that kindness and sense of right, he won't need your dos and do nots.

Please, mission school, teach him the learnings of man.

Do not teach him to think he is learning religion—or he'll think what he had before was not religion.

Please, you have a precious property in one of those third floor rows of bunks.

Good things came from this writing. A priest at that very mission school had recently changed his profession to teaching at a university. He taught and wrote a book about the Lakota wisdom, and was developing curriculum and teachers with sensitivity to the great wisdom Fools Crow and other elders had imparted to him.

My ex-husband wrote me he'd read of a job opening at the USD Indian Ed. Dept. where Dr. John Bryde was undergoing his amazing transformation.

I walked into Bryde's office and gave him the above writing about Billy. He read it, looked at me long and hard, and hired me. I would write second grade readers based on harmony with earth, each other, creator, and self. The characters in the books would show the Lakota traits of bravery, doing a hard thing without complaining, sharing, and freedom of choice to follow one's own inner voice, but choose with concern for what is the best for the people. I later published in my magazine Bryde's "reasons for temporarily relinquishing the sacramental exercise of the priesthood . . . I can no longer be an official voice in forcing and regulating an individual's response to God."

Something soon happened at the mission school, and on a week-end trip back to the ranch, I happily found Billy Pawnee Leggins was back with his beloved old people.

And now it was time to let the readers of my magazine know what was happening to their associate editor under the care of Frank and Kate.

Your associate editor's new name is Winyan. You can pronounce it Wea, if you'd like, if you'll give the "e" a nasal sound. The most perfect pronunciation I heard outdoors long ago from a bird or insect. Perhaps one of you will recognize the species with that call and write letting us know.

Winyan, in Lakota, means woman.

The rest of the name will be given after a year of purification, and a mid-June vision quest (hanbleceya) supervised by Lakota (Sioux) holy man Frank Fools Crow.

In the meantime, words and thoughts of pessimism are to be replaced by optimism, in joy and pain. Humble admission of areas of ignorance is to replace braggery. Swearing is out—replaced by silence until perspective is regained. (There are no swear words in Lakota.) Gossip is to be replaced by good will toward all.

Accountability is up to one's self.

Interestingly, no matter how firm the inward resolution to change, nothing makes quite the impact of example.

It was early, chilly early, when Frank and Kate Fools Crow and I set out in a loaded, bulging VW for the Ft. Yates, N.D., powwow. It was to be a four day trip, and a tent would be set up for us by the people who had requested Frank come and attend their daughter with his medicine and prayer.

These four days were to have a purifying impact no amount of resolution could have brought about.

There is something about poking your nose out of a warm sleeping bag into a chilly North Dakota 6:30 a.m. that makes you want to forget about trying to become a Lakota, or trying to become, period. Especially if you are not the rise and shine type.

There is something about catching a glimpse of a shivering and quiet 75-year-old Kate reaching into sacks of groceries picking out things for breakfast, and knowing she's too gentle and polite to poke the sleepyhead with the green Coleman and ask her to get it lit. As you watch her you begin to care again.

One thing that was not purifying was four days of my cooking. Frank's and Kate's 76-and 75-year old systems came through it fine. My 28-year-old system after three days, utterly renounced my boasts of rugged outdoorsmanship.

And that was the day of the big night of the powwow. The two previous nights, I'd just begun to get the feel—the total mind, spirit, body involvement—of the dance. The first attempt had been in one of Kate's gloriously colored blankets and my moccasins, with pieces of cardboard protecting the two half-dollar-sized areas of my feet that the moccasins had once protected. The second attempt had been in Kate's red-beaded, tasseled blanket and a lovely new pair of moccasins quietly handed to me by a lady I'd jokingly showed my holey moccasins the night before. I have since learned to be careful about making my needs known to the Indian people, lest into my hands come an underserved treasure.

But here it was, the big third night and I felt more like dancing off a cliff than around the powwow circle. It's hard to listen to your stomach, though, when all around is building the tension of the 1968 dance championship contest. This would be the night

Frank would put on his full regalia and headdress which would say to all what the caption said under the color photo in "National Geographic"—Chief Frank Fools Crow.

The graceful, large eagle feathers which made up the headdress had special meaning to me. For from my sacred pipe's stem (my first attempt at carving) hung a feather that was from the headdress eagle. And one of that eagle's claws (eagle claws are unobtainable, I'd been informed by a museum keeper) hung on a necklace that was my first attempt at beadwork. The necklace had been finished shortly before we made ready to enter the powwow grounds.

Dramatic is not the word, there is none, for the mood of the moment. Kate was majestic-stately in her soft doe skin dress and ankle-high all-beaded moccasins. Frank was fully Chief that night. He is a kind man with a sharp wit and we joke a lot. But when he puts on that headdress he feels and he accepts that responsibility. And anyone who accompanies him feels and accepts that responsibility.

The reporter in me wishes I'd been on the outside looking in as this regal couple entered and found a seat, placing between them a strange combination, of sunburn, freckles, light-brown braids, and blanket.

The drums had been beating for some time before the inside-out stomach returned to mind.

Drums have anesthetic power, it seems, as well as energizing power. For as I looked into the moving splendor of color and motion and life, I saw the lady who had entertained and fed us before the people got our tent up. The lady who, for the hour it took at the stove, needed two in bed to ease the pain in her leg. She was dancing.

There was something purifying about her example
And deep.
The Native American dance means total involvement.
The dance of life means total involvement.

As I joined the moving splendor of color and motion and life, I knew I had a long way to go.

The magazine "Great Plains Observer" with this article was one of two I was putting out. The Presbyterian Synod of South Dakota had asked me to edit their "Dakota Heartbeat." One editorial used the symbol of Mobil Oil's flying red horse. The editorial said that there were four horses in a run for their lives. The red horse held back and watched. When he could see the other horses were in trouble, he put on excellent speed, and led them to safety. Soon the synod had elected a quiet, wise, leader from the tribe for which their state was named.

Chapter Two

"Winyan, come with me," the voice said. I got up from my vision quest square marked off by tobacco offerings at the top of Bear Butte. I threw off my blanket and followed. It was a caring voice, so I trusted.

"You did throw off your blanket and run down the hill, but your hair was black," another vision quester told me later.

It was June 1969. I had gone through my year of purification. Frank Fools Crow had gathered three of us together, we stopped at a store for blankets and tobacco offerings, and he sent us up Bear Butte. This is the hill near Sturgis, South Dakota, where Crazy Horse fasted. He stayed at the bottom of the hill to pray for us.

He talked about that hanbleciyapi in the book *Fools Crow*, by Thomas Mails.

"The occasion of my greatest vision experience at Bear Butte. Three white people—an older man, a younger man, and a young girl—came to my home to see me, and wanted me to take them on a vision quest. I held the sweat lodge ceremony with them, and took them to Bear Butte. I got them situated in vision-questing places at the top, and came back down to the meadow, where I made my camp.

"The Cheyenne had built a sweat lodge in the center of the meadow and the willow framework was still standing there. So I covered it over, got everything ready, and went into the sweat lodge to be with the white people in prayer and spirit. I intended to remain there for the four nights and days, and to ask Wakan-Tanka and Grandfather to answer their needs. But as I was praying on the fourth night, a voice interrupted me and told me to come out. I crawled outside the lodge and stood up. I was wearing only a breechclout and was barefooted; I had my pipe in my hand. It was about 3:00 a.m., and it was quite cold, so I put my buffalo robe

over my shoulders and wrapped it around my body in the ancient way . . . .

"I looked around and saw no one. But I did as I was told. I prayed to Grandfather, saying I had come there as the voice told me to, and then I knocked on what appeared to be a wooden door in the face of the rock wall. The door swung slowly open and I could see inside. It was pitch black in there, and I was trembling. So I took only three or four nervous steps inside and stopped. The door closed behind me, and I began immediately to thank Grandfather for answering my prayers. I thanked him passionately for healing people through me, and for the confidence I had that he would help us find a solution to the drinking problem that was plaguing our reservation. I asked him to guide me and to keep me humble. I asked him to help me, because our people needed help. And still being afraid, I reminded him that I had a wife and a daughter to go back to.

"When I finished my prayer, a voice answered in perfect Lakota 'When you go back, take some of your first meal, whether it is small or large, and throw some away. Do this to show how much you love your people and how willing you are to give yourself. We know you have never exaggerated or boasted, or kept anything from your people. You have lived the life that was planned for you. We know when you are sad and we know when you are happy . . . .

"I don't know how long I was actually inside the cliff—perhaps ten minutes, perhaps fifteen. Anyway, when I came out, I heard voices of many people, both children and adults, laughing and talking in the Lakota language. They made many happy sounds. I did not see them, but I could tell their ages by the sound of their voices. I began to rub my eyes and when I looked and listened again, there was nothing. Not even a sound could be heard now. I looked at the place where the door had been, and it was just solid rock. So I climbed with some difficulty down the cliff and returned to the sweat lodge in the meadow.

"As impossible as it seems, I believe now that one day prayers about the liquor problem on the reservation will be answered. The closed and vanished door was a final thing, showing me there would be an end to it, and the happy people represented the Teton people, who will be joyful once again when the liquor is gone. That time has not yet come but many Sioux detest drinking and liquor today and we are making progress . . ."

Fools Crow went on to say he got the power to talk to birds and animals after that vision quest.

When I returned to the sacred square after being called away as mentioned at the beginning of this chapter, I had the feeling I had been in a cave. I felt very relaxed and filled with peace. I went to sleep and received the following vision.

A Native American was walking along a road. He came upon a black man lying by the road. He stopped to help and heal him and found that the man had amnesia. He had once known the spirit ways, but kidnapping, slave ships, and slavery had caused him to forget them. Once reminded, the black man became strong again in spirit very quickly. The two walked on down the road together. They came across a white man lying beside the road. They stopped to help him, but he was so steeped in materialism and man-made things that it took both of them and all their energy to teach him the spirit ways.

When the older man, young man, and I came down the hill, Fools Crow was waiting for us. He was glowing. He said he could give me my name now. I was very humbled and honored by the name he gave me.

In Mail's *Fools Crow*, the holy man states, "When a person is right with God he always has a special feeling. When I am curing I feel a charge of power and I am excited! I know about these things because they are going on inside of me. When people come to me for help, for an ailment or curing or whatever, as I do my ceremony I feel the strength, the energy building up. And I know I can cure them. The spirits let me know it. They even come inside of me and give me confidence and strength. And I feel good about this as it builds up inside of me."

This energy of Fools Crow was obvious to me when, after the vision quest, I returned to the reservation to camp out as I had the year before, and to drive Fools Crow to heal people. After one very long trip, in which I was exhausted on return and collapsed in my tent, I saw a car drive up and the people request Fools Crows' help. The holy man, nearing 80, got in the car, went to the sand hills of Nebraska and healed again. He was vibrant with energy upon return the next day. The more he gave out his energy, the more was poured into him. I saw the same at Yuipi ceremonies. He literally glowed from his closeness to the creative force of our universe.

Thomas Mails here quotes Fools Crow in the book titled by the great medicine man's name.

"The true medicine person and the holy person do not try to cheat, to just get by, or to fool anyone. Instead they are the ones that always work and study the hardest. As long as we have the strength to do Wakan Tanka's will, we work at our job constantly. Although we keep our lives in balance, we don't waste time. People can do anything if they want to do it badly enough. Of course, medicine people must take the time to actually experience things to know how they truly are. Can we know how rain or snow feels without being out in it? Can we know how a Sun Dance feels without experiencing what a dancer does? Can we know about suffering if we don't suffer? Another thing medicine people need is a good sense of humor. You know that I enjoy life and like to laugh. Laughter breaks the tension. It is a very good healer. And it keeps us from taking life too seriously. After all, Wakan Tanka and the Helpers are the Chiefs of the ages. They have always been, and always will be. We come and go, but the sacred hoop was turning before us, and if we do what Wakan Tanka wishes us to do, it will keep turning after we are gone."

His reference to the Helpers strikes a very familiar chord. At my first vision quest on Bear Butte the year before, I had an experience that taught me never to feel alone. I was surrounded by Helpers. Plants and a tree vibrated with love. The stone I would later take to Fools Crow glowed. Four stars fell, one moved. Alone? Never again.

Regarding his sense of humor, the insight I got into that was on a long trip back from Lame Deer, Montana. I was driving the VW, Frank was in the passenger seat, and Kate in back with the healing and sacred parcels. No matter how long the trip and how crowded, they never complained. But we must have all been a little travel weary because the following hilarious argument took place.

Winyan: Did you see that car with the woman driving and the deer on top?

Frank: Two deer on top.

Winyan: One deer on top.

Frank: Two deer on top.

Winyan: Okay. Two deer on top. Woman shot both deer.

Frank and Kate laughed long over that. How could you not love them both?

When we got home, my tent had blown down and ripped to shreds. I wrote the following for my magazine about how the old couple knew me better than I knew myself. And how to get me to live up to it.

Winyan lay on sun-parched grass
Beside a tent
A tent sewn for an Iowa woods
Not a Dakota prairie
The seams had ripped to shreds.

The sun beat down,
A will began to wilt.
Weakened by flu
And without money
To buy another tent

Winyan lay on the sun-parched grass.
A mirage appeared.
A lake, cool and lovely,
Would welcome her
The people there take care of her

"Winyan," a voice cut into her brooding,
"Winyan, you must come help
Lift paralyzed daughter
Into car."
Winyan got to her feet

The movement jarred
Her stomach
She excused herself to some trees.
Then joined the moving.

The Oglala woman had not walked
For years
Only her hands could move
To bead
Only her face could move
To smile and laugh

To wince and cry out
Only when they moved her
And touched her foot to something hard
To smile if a puppy lay on it.

The Oglala woman was in the car
Winyan's eyes had changed.
She got needle and thread
And went to the tent
And sat on the sun-parched grass.

All day she sat.
The sun beat down.
Her teeth and fingers worked.
And the next day
She only knew her teeth and fingers worked.

Again the tent was up.
The Lakota way.
It had faced the north.
Now it faced the east.
Now Winyan faced the east.

And the example of Kate and Frank was powerful. Frank told Thomas Mails about where he got his vast energy and optimism.

"I have been told about the Fountain of Youth. But that is only a dream. If people really want to stay healthy and live a long time, there is a real way to do it. They must give themselves to Wakan Tanka (Great Spirit) and live a spiritual life. They will have the peace that frees them from fear. They will know that Wakan Tanka and the Helpers surround them, and that nothing can hurt them that they can't recover from. So there is no fear. They remain calm, and they are unhurried. They do not get ulcers or have sudden heart attacks while they are still young. I have had a couple, but I was eighty-five before I had the first one. Spiritual people do not suffer as much from anxiety as other people do, and they do not worry as much about being chiefs or pleasing others just to get ahead in life. Instead, the things they do are personally rewarding. They feel good about themselves and they naturally take care of themselves as they ought to."

I was beginning to understand this "live for the people," concept. Fools Crows beautiful granddaughter told me this story as we sat sewing in the tent one day. I had seen her haul water to the house and do the laundry and I was so impressed with her love for Frank and Kate, I commented on it. But by the time she finished her story, I understood many things much better. She had been given a home with some wealthy people and moved to St. Louis. There she lived in luxury and had all the material things she could ever want. It was empty, she said. There was no need for her, nothing to live for. She remembered Kate and Frank and all that they were living for and she wanted to be with them, helping any way she could.

On a trip with us later, she and another teenager would teach me how deeply embedded into the Lakota child is the "live for the people" truth.

I wrote the following for my magazine "Great Plains Observer" after a powerful weekend at a powwow.

It was May and the earth was coming to life.

A dedicated Lakota holy man and his quiet, loyal wife were where they should be—even in their nearing 80 years.

At a powwow.

The circle, the unity, of the Lakota comes together so seldom now compared to the constant circle of tipis of their childhood memories, that they need to be there.

My VW, boasting its own 150,000 miles of age, had glowed a little while carrying these people to the Montana powwow from their Pine Ridge Reservation home.

As two of the holy couple's granddaughters and I sat in the VW outside the hall, the loud drumbeat surrounded us. That drumbeat was beginning to be part of me, but I realized I could never sacrifice as much of my eighty years to keep it beating as the man and woman who were inside—who were as close to it as a soul to a heartbeat.

Laryngitis and other flu symptoms had kept me out of moccasins and shawl tonight. As I sat reading a newly purchased book, CRAZY HORSE, STRANGE MAN OF THE OGLALAS, I half listened to the conversation of the granddaughters, who were interested in a white-style dance going on across town.

A shame, I thought. And with typical white capacity of sticking in nose where not invited, I mustered up my raspy voice and asked why the girls did not powwow dance. Why they liked white dances.

"Because we're teenagers," they retorted. And on reflection I was glad they did not let me or anyone else run their lives.

Soon I was to find that the frug, twist, or today's latest dance could not take a Lakota-ness out of them. A Lakota-ness much deeper than the wearing of moccasins or shawl would have testified to.

I'd been sitting there reading of the great Lakota, Crazy Horse.

It was a book of hardship, struggle, and sacrifice.

I read on.

It was a book of more hardship, more struggle, and more sacrifice.

I read on.

The strange man, Crazy Horse, decided, in his young adulthood, to assume the ultimate hardship. To let this crisis period of his people flow not over him or around him, but right through his guts. To bear the pain of everyone in the circle.

But there was a woman he loved. He'd brushed flies from her face when she was an infant in the cradle board.

She loved him also.

Out of family obedience, she married another. Later, with Lakota womanhood's freedom to leave an unhappy marriage, she became, briefly, the wife of the strange, quiet leader.

Resulting jealousy threatened to tear apart the Lakota in this time when unity alone would bring victory in a world seething with the white enemy.

He returned her—and the heir he longed for, and she longed to give him. With the vermillion circles of one loved on her cheeks, the braids he'd braided . . .

I threw the book down.

I'd had it.

I could take reading of his hardship, his struggles, and his sacrifices.

But the sacrifice of a life-giving love let die—I muttered some good washichu (white) curses. There are no profane words in Lakota.

And then I raised my laryngitis-inflicted voice to benefit the two teen-age granddaughters of the holy couple—to benefit them with my opinion of the sacrificing nature of Crazy Horse.

There was silence for a moment after my tirade.

Then one of these "teen-age" girls spoke very simply.

"Did he do it for his people?"

It wasn't hard to find Kate in the crowd. And I didn't deserve her typical obliging of my request for a shawl.

I certainly didn't deserve what she came through with. Frank's ceremonial robe.

I did not deserve to join this circle of the long-suffering relatives of the great Itanca (leader) I'd been reading about.

Just as I do not deserve to take the holy communion of the long-suffering Christ.

All the "good deeds" or suffering in the world would never make me deserve to be a part of these people who stood their test.

But every living thing has some type of heartbeat. and every living thing struggles to become.

That was enough for Kate and Frank, who saw so clearly how far I had to go.

It was enough for the people in that circle who let me dance with them to that ever-increasing, ever-expanding drumbeat.

Later, after Eagle Man introduced me to Long Elk, I re-read Sandoz' *Crazy Horse, Strange Man of the Oglalas*, I found the reference to Spotted Tail's daughter marrying the French trapper. The couple were listed in Rosebud tribal records as the ancestors of Long Elk. So I knew he was also related to Crazy Horse whose mother was sister to Spotted Tail. And when she died, another sister of Spotted Tail raised him. And when Crazy Horse and his people were forced onto a reservation after the battle at Little Big Horn, Crazy Horse took his family to Spotted Tail for protection. Then Crazy Horse was killed when he resisted being locked up. During his vision quest on Bear Butte, he had been told no white man's bullet could hurt him and he had ridden through much of their fire.

Spotted Tail also was a brave warrior and after a battle, an officer said if he would turn himself in, sacrificing himself for his people, they would be treated well. To certain death he thought he was going, when he was taken to Fort Leavenworth, in Kansas. What he saw was worse than death. Unending numbers of troops and settlers. The idea of his people dying in front of cannons, was worse than the reservation that was forced on them. But when he returned to his people he picked reservation land far from the Missouri River where blankets with small pox were being given to the Lakota. Rosebud has river, lake, and forests.

Long Elk was born and raised at a dance hall on a lake on Spotted Tail's Rosebud Reservation. His father was Irish and his mother was of the blood of not only Oglala Crazy Horse, and Brule Spotted Tail, but also of Sitting Bull's co-chief Gall. Sitting Bull and Gall were Hunkpapa, another of the great Teton Lakota groups. So Grandpa Joe Gordon helped to raise Long Elk and to impress on this eldest grandson his bloodline and responsibilities for his people.

His grandfather told him he would be reported killed in three wars, but he would come back. A woman would bead his name in black and red, he would lead her to her destiny, and he would die.

Born in 1922, he was of Marine Corps fighter pilot age in World War II and was shot down in Japan. He evaded capture due to intense training and testing by Grandpa Joe.

Over Korea, in that next war, he was shot down and captured. For 18 months in North Korea, he was tortured, but helped others evade signing false confessions or giving up. Tied up in an isolated cave for months, he had to hide tears, because seeing them would make his captors think he was near to breaking and torture him even more. During this time, Grandpa Joe appeared to him to keep him sane.

As troop carriers were loading up prisoners after the truce, his captors said he must confess to war crimes, or they would keep him. He told them to keep him then. The photo of him being released and shaking hands with an American officer is of a near skeleton whose face is glowing. The p.o.w.s were sent home on ships rather than airplanes to have time to prepare them. The doctors tried to get Long Elk to hate his torturers and he refused. "If they were doing it because they were forced to, I feel sorry for them. If they were doing it because they enjoyed it, I feel sorry for them."

During the Vietnam war he was a passenger in a military plane that crashed in U.S. mountains. He saved the other passengers using knowledge of rescue methods and skills of survival. But Grandpa Joe had been right. The third death notice was entered into his file.

When Long Elk told me these things it was from one whose eyes showed great pain to another whose eyes showed great pain. My mother's mental illness had caused her to physically abuse me and lock me in closets. But in adulthood, I got her the help she needed.

Maybe all of this is why Grandpa Joe saw me as the woman who would give him a beaded band of his warrior colors, black and red, blood and death.

One day, when I was waiting for Long Elk and he didn't come, I started to feel sorry for myself. Grandpa Joe put in my mind the thoughts "Self-pity is not a worthy thing. Bead him something."

I had a bowl of multi-colored beads, but I must have been in a type of trance because I put Long in red beads on a black background and Elk in black on a red background. ("You will return and a woman will give you a beaded band with your name in black and red, (blood and death). You'll lead her to her destiny, and you will die.")

When I gave it to him, he dropped it like a hot coal. "Where did you get this?" he accused. Tearing up, I said "Grandpa Joe told me to bead it for you." I couldn't understand, because he had been so kind until that moment.

He went to his holy hill, came back, and this time he accepted the beaded band and told me the prophecy and why he had rejected the beaded band.

That was February, 1969. Many other sacred signs were given to us.

In November, 1978, nine years later, I called him from Alaska. His voice and his heart condition were barely able to say his last words to me. "We (as society) need more unity. We need more unity." He died on St. Patrick's Day in 1979.

His last years were partly spent doing stained glass including for a church. He did the stations of the cross, and in dedicating them at the church he said, as torture increases, and pain gets worse, you lose the ability to see color. So the first steel and glass stations were done in color, the last in black and white. By then, Christ was unable to see color.

Chapter Three

As I write this chapter in 2005, and look back at my 65 years, I have worked at a number of jobs. They range from news reporter, to waitress and dishwasher, to construction secretary for an oil company in Alaska, to teaching.

How many times I would look back on the years of 1968 and 1969, just mentioned. Then came 1970 to 1972 and I would draw power from all these years. To stand on a mountain amid powerful people, signs, and visions, and then go back to being a white woman working nine to five again was not easy.

The years 1970, 1971, and 1972, according to the stone, 9-2-4 and 8 started with February gatherings of four races. My Cherokee lady friend was dating an Asian American and I was dating his black friend that Feb. 14, 1970. This would start the series of Februarys when black, white, yellow, and red would appear.

I was showing the black friend my stone with the four trees. He held one side as I held the other, and he said a current of electricity flowed through as when touching an electric knob at a carnival. That had happened before as a friend and I held my Sacred Pipe, so I was not surprised.

A month later, Fools Crow told me to begin to get ready for a Yuipi ceremony to be held for me at the University of South Dakota in Vermillion. My Cherokee lady friend was there grounding me as Fools Crow tied tightly in his robe, began to pray inside a circle of tobacco ties of black, white, red and yellow. When he was untied by his spirit guides, he was given a Yuipi stone to give me. This protection stone was usually given to Lakota warriors. I was so humbled as he handed it to me, I wept for several moments until my friend told me sharply, "enough."

Later, I asked Fools Crow what was said as the spirits told him to give me the stone. "Tell her she will be hated by white and

Indian. Whatever group she works with the others will not like it. But tell her to hold the stone in her right hand toward the heavens and anything she needs will be given." I wore it in a leather pouch and though I have not always had all I wanted or thought I needed, I have always had all I really needed.

The next February found me in Oaxaca (wa-ha-ca) Mexico under the world's oldest living tree. Ancestor to the giant redwoods, it dwarfed the cathedral beside it, which was crumbling. The tree was still emerald green with life. When the third tree and I arrived on Feb. 2, 1971, the ancient blessing of the seed was taking place amid bands playing.

Red Horse's Fire was a Lakota raised in urban Denver. He skipped school to go to the public library to read about Native American people. When the truant officer came after him, the librarian testified that he had spent those school hours in her library. One thing he was researching was the Zapotec people, and the Sun Bowl, or Aztec Calendar.

I later learned that Benito Juarez, an early president of Mexico, was a Zapotec shepherd boy from the hills who had to promise to be a priest to get a Catholic education. The third tree liked to quote this great man. "Respect for the rights of others is the peace," Juarez said.

Red Horse's Fire learned in his reading at the library that the Zapotec (People of the Clouds) had a sacred place in Oaxaca, Mexico, where Quetzalcoatl had meditated and called four men from four directions to meet and learn of sacred things.

The young Lakota became fascinated with the Aztec calendar and its 52 year cycles. From it came a prophecy of 13 heaven cycles, ending with the arrival of Cortez, and nine hell cycles to end in 1987. When I met him he was putting all this in a book. He was writing *LORD OF THE DAWN, QUETZALCOATL*. As Lord of the Dawn, the ancient spiritual leader had sent word via four men to four directions to prepare for the dawn.

Six months later, the stone's 8, August 1971, found me teaching from that book to my English students at Highmore, South Dakota, High School. On Aug. 27, there appeared, in one day, in my classroom, in this small ranch town, people from the four colors and four directions. A Nigerian exchange student, a Japanese exchange teacher, and one of my Lakota students, plus the white students. We did a ceremony of presenting the colors of the four directions by the four races. Then we read from the book.

Later, the superintendent came in as I was closing down for the night, and I said, "What kind of a school are you running, where you teach a piece of literature and it immediately comes true in the classroom?" I threw a piece of chalk directly above me and it splattered on the floor, for an exclamation point. He smiled at me and said, "The kind of school where teachers pay for the broken chalk."

That weekend, Fools Crow honored me by letting me give a flesh offering in the Pine Ridge Sun Dance. In a leather shirt I had beaded and a leather skirt covered with Kate's blanket, I held the sacred pipe Fools Crow had given me as I joined the other sun dancers. I was honored to join the first tree on the stone and many other men and women who were pierced and gave flesh offerings. Two small pieces of upper arm were placed in the ground at the foot of the sacred cottonwood Sun Dance tree. I was proud then, and later, when, over the loud speaker after the ceremony, the first tree, Eagle Man, quoted an editorial I'd written. It told of outrage at priests intervening in the Sun Dance, which they did again that year. "We Lakota people would never consider coming into your church on your holiest Christmas Eve and start telling you how to celebrate."

I noticed the tears of gratitude of the many Lakota who filed past the sun dancers after the ceremony. Each Lakota was grateful to the dancers who had pledged their piercing so healing would come to a sick person. And they were grateful to them for keeping the old ways alive.

Before the piercing and flesh offering, we had each presented our sacred pipe to one of the many holy men. John Fire accepted mine. He later told me on a visit to his Rosebud Reservation home that one day a black, white, red, and yellow Crazy Horse, carrying a black catlinite pipe would lead the world. It fit with the experiences I had been having of the appearance of the four races during the 9-2-4-8 holy months.

The next February, 1972, found me in the South Dakota Senate chamber, where Long Elk had won a seat, the first Lakota to serve in the state legislature. I sat up in the balcony reading of his ancestor, Sinte Gleska (Spotted Tail), uncle of Crazy Horse. Long Elk, below, had been blessed with all that leadership blood and was sometimes overwhelmed with the responsibility of getting it as a young boy. It weighed on him and he felt he had failed. When I agreed to take up the burden and help his people, some of the stress left, and he literally looked younger.

His grandfather, who had passed it to him as the eldest grandson, had told him, as mentioned before in this book, that he would reported killed while serving in three wars, but nothing could kill him. Then he would meet a woman who would bead his name in black and red. He would lead her to her destiny and he would die. He had, in 1969, told me this days after I gave him the beaded band and he threw it down, not wanting to touch it.

Now, as he served in the Senate in Pierre, S.D., near where I'd taught school, he assured me that after he died he would help me from the spirit world. He explained that while in the North Korean concentration camp for 18 months, his grandfather had appeared to him and helped him. "I can do that for you, warning you," he said and smiled toward where a pizza was burning.

The last day of February 1972, a leap year 29th, one of my last times to see the second tree, he brought me a message from Sitting Bull about his return, the second message. The first had been in November, 1969, as he showed me where Sitting Bull had been buried before the Lakota moved him to where he could never be found.

So now I knew both the powerful chiefs would come back to lead.

This was all restated in a maximum security prison in Stillwater, Minnesota, on August 27, 1972. On that date, August 27, in 1969, Lake Poinsett water had stilled around Wanblee Witco, a Rosebud Lakota, as he had told the restless waves to be calm. Then he came to where I was putting out my magazine in nearby Madison and told me of this new sign among all I had been given. So I was amazed to find myself at Stillwater prison on that exact date three years later. The fourth tree on the stone recognized me dressed in black, white, red and yellow and wearing the honored black Apache blanket Fools Crow had given me. This Apache-Lakota graduate physicist and Marine pilot was serving a sentence for rescuing the bones of a sacred Minnesota Dakota chief from a museum.

I was writing curriculum for the St. Paul (Minnesota) Public Schools Indian Ed. Dept. One project was to put into a book the speeches Winnebago elder Henry Green Crow gave to school children. He had a wonderful speech pattern which I kept in his printed stories. Someone else in the department decided to "correct" it. That copy disappeared, my supervisor told me. It would be like "correcting" Uncle Remus. Soon elementary school teachers were telling me that reading the stories to the children was like having Henry there talking to them.

These things I talked about with Wolf of Yukon in the prison. Also, he was told of, and he told me of the return of Sitting Bull and Crazy Horse. This was the third person who had told me of this.

Wolf of Yukon urged me to go to his pristine land in Alaska and the Yukon where the old ways were still alive. And he told me of a legend a Blue Eyes would bring the Sacred Pipe to his Athabascan people.

So in 1975 I headed north with a graduate assistantship at the U. of Alaska, Fairbanks, where I would develop Native curriculum and take Alaska Native languages and anthropology.

Chapter Four

The Alaska journey started in Stillwater State Prison in Minnesota in the early 1970s. The fourth tree had spoken of his unspoiled land.

Since Fools Crow had given me a sacred pipe, it didn't surprise me when Wolf (that was his spirit guide and Athabascan name) was told by his Yukon Territory parents, he had met Blue Eyes. She and a wolf would take the sacred pipe to his Athabascan people.

Years passed and I was working for a bush airline in Fairbanks, Alaska. I was ticket agent and our passengers were Athabascans from the villages near Fairbanks. As a fringe benefit I was allowed to hop aboard and fly to the villages.

I had heard the people speak very respectfully of the Athabascan elder, Johnny Frank of Venetie. They spoke with the same awe and admiration as the Lakota for another Frank—Fools Crow.

Then, one day I heard Johnny Frank was in the hospital in a coma. I got the pipe Fools Crow had given me and went to his room. I sat quietly for a long time. Then I began to pray with the pipe. When I was finished, still in his coma, he raised his right arm to the sky as Frank Fools Crow had taught me to do when I pray.

Soon after, his daughter came in and we talked. I left believing he had heard me.

By 1978, ten cycles starting with 9 had passed. More and more I was meeting all four races during the cycles. But none more dramatically than I met them the day my son was born on September 3. The anesthesiologist was Asian American, the nurses were black and Native American, and the doctor was white. His father, Montana born and Alaska raised, and I married in a sacred pipe ceremony on a beautiful hill looking down on the Tanana River in Fairbanks, Alaska.

I cannot express how overjoyed I was that the month on my stone, 9, had brought me my greatest joy yet. And my son and I still find ourselves experiencing and learning, and always will.

In 1985, in our Wasilla, Alaska, apartment, I read my son a Hans Christian Anderson fairy tale. I began thinking, "I can do that." Thoughts returned about the legend of a wolf and a woman bringing the sacred pipe to the Athabascans.

SILVER

Once in the far north, a mother wolf and her pup, who had been sick, looked out at the cold December day.

"Why do we get sick, Mother?" asked the pup.

"So we will appreciate being healthy, perhaps."

"But last month you told me that. Why did I have to get sick again?" the pup asked.

"So you would get some rest perhaps."

The pup eyed his mother. He was starting to question whether mothers know everything after all. He ventured out into the world a little further. His body was still a great burden for his unsteady legs, but he had to know more.

"Who makes us get sick?" he asked his mother.

"We do, we tell our bodies what to do and they do whatever we tell them."

Now he knew the old lady had slipped a cog.

"I did not tell my body to get sick!"

The mother wolf looked at her pup. All the thousands of mothers in the world had looked that way. How much can he understand was written on her patient, loving face, proud of her son for asking.

"You have complete control—and if you don't like what your mind is ordering your body to do, change the orders."

"Oh."

The pup yawned and decided to go looking for his father.

"I'll be back," he said.

"Okay, you know your boundaries."

Exhausted, she was glad for the rest before another of her brood woke up.

Silver usually could find his father where he stood watching mice nests for movement. There was a great deal of caution in

Silver's awkward step so his father would not lose prey because of a noisy pup's step.

"Father"

"Yes, son"

"Is this what I will do when I grow up?"

"No, my son."

"What will I do?"

"You will leave this hill, your brothers and parents to carry something important to some people."

"How do you know?"

"Your mother told me."

"Does she know very much?"

"Oh, yes."

"More than you?"

"She teaches me and I teach her. She was told about you long before you came to us."

"Who told her about me?"

"A young Native American man met her along the trail and was very, very sick, wounded and hungry. He'd got lost and your mother hunted for him until he got better."

"Oh." Silver sat quietly for a few minutes and thought about all of this.

"What are Native Americans?"

"They walk on two legs instead of four, but in all other ways they are our brothers. They respect our life and territory and we respect theirs."

"Can they talk to us?"

"Those who have spirit ways can."

"What are spirit ways?"

"Spirit is a force field that unites and tunes in on others on the same wave length."

"Did he come here with Mother?"

"No. I did not know your mother then. She came here later because he told her about our great quiet hills where we are as we were created to be."

"Is it like this everyplace?"

"No, he met your mother in a terrible place where people shoot at people and animals and fight over land and money."

Silver was tired and the hot sun felt warm on his fur, so he rolled over and let it warm his belly. He couldn't imagine anyplace but what he'd known. Love surrounding him from all directions.

Maybe tomorrow he'd ask more. What was it his father had said? He must carry something someplace?

When he awakened, the sun was sinking and his father had accumulated quite a pile of mice Silver would help carry home for supper.

That night the full moon was shining on his mother and he noticed something glimmer from under her thick neck fur. He asked her about it.

"A Native American gave it to me," she said.

"What is it?"

"One day it will be yours."

He looked closely at it and it shone in the moonlight and had something scratched onto it.

"Was it the Native American you found and helped?"

"That is right."

"So he gave you that?"

"Yes, son."

"Oh. That is what I must carry to someone."

"No. But it will help you find those people and your mission."

Silver had more interest right then in the pressing problem of a brother about to get a caribou bone Silver had not quite finished off. The fight soon over, he enjoyed a friendly romp with his brothers to the stream.

On the way there, a tremendous shaking of the earth began and when they tried to return, the earth in front of them opened up into a big gap. It swallowed his three brothers, and Silver barely leaped across it clawing his way to keep from being swallowed up.

When he got to the den, he saw his father standing over his mother's body, which he had dragged from the cave that had collapsed on her. Silver didn't ask his father why she lay so still. His spirit, some kind of force field, told him.

He looked at the thing around her neck, gleaming in the yellow, heartless moonlight that had watched all this terror.

His father's nudging and caressing began to slow now. A great noise from somewhere deep in his father finally was released.

Silver went to his father and only then realized now broken his father's body also was.

His frightened eyes met the old wise one's eyes and the son saw more pain than he'd seen before. Pain of love and pain of body.

The old one moved awkwardly to his mate's head and took the chain in his teeth, lifted it from around her neck and put it on his son.

His eyes were gentle now and full of the look of pride all sons crave to see in their father's eyes.

"You will do fine, my son," the eyes told him.

Silver waited through the long, quiet night beside his father. He didn't sleep. He brought the mice they'd been eating. But his father wouldn't eat. In the morning he made one last great effort to comfort his son and give him the wisdom he would need to complete the prophecy.

"Soon you must begin on your journey to find the Native American brother of your mother, my son. On the way you will pass through four villages where you will be recognized and loved. The first, a village of black people, the second, a village of white people, the third, a village of Asian American people and then the village of the Native American who put the chain on your mother."

The old wolf was very weak now and Silver knew he was getting ready to enter the spirit world. But the great power that the old wolf had shown in his life, was now shining through his eyes so filled with pride in Silver.

So many times in the days ahead, Silver would want to give up. But that love and pride of his father would keep his feet moving. He could not prove unworthy.

But now the time had come for the tired father to join his mate and Silver's brothers, in their new spirit life where they would watch Silver fulfill the prophecy.

Silver was still a pup. But the nature of a pup is to survive no matter the odds. Silver could not bear to leave, but he could not bear to stay either. He would set off, he decided, and find his mother's Native American brother.

He was unaccustomed to having anything around his neck and since his mother's neck was larger than his, it dragged a bit as he walked.

The hills looked strange. Trees had fallen, rocks had leaped out of the earth, others had fallen into great cracks.

Many days had passed and Silver had gotten leaner and hungrier when he came to the village of the black people. He felt at home there, because an eight-year-old boy named Justin adopted him. Silver was immediately aware of these people's great strength, intelligence, and sensitivity. He didn't know how, but he sensed that he had been there before, that they knew him and he had once lived among them.

The same feeling of something familiar came to him in the white village. A young boy named Nathan took him home to his family which included him in their Christmas celebration and gave him the feeling that he was part of their family. Nathan even hung up a Christmas stocking on Christmas Eve which Santa filled with bones for Silver.

And in the Asian American village, Ming Li took him to her house to enjoy the Buddhist traditions and eat some wonderful foods from Asia.

Language doesn't confuse a wolf like it does the two-leggeds. He looks deep into people and hears from their tone of voice if they are friend or foe.

But it was something more than instinct. He could follow at the heels of the wise ones of all races and recognize their celebrations, adapt to their houses and play the children's games, with a sense of having done it before.

That mystery was about to be solved—for at last he was about to meet his mother's Native American brother.

Months had passed now, and his size had grown to match that of his now dimly-remembered parents. He was strong, with heavy, thick neck fur that hid the chain he'd grown to fit.

As he entered the village, a young girl noticed him first and got some food for him. When he'd eaten, she gently looked at the chain. She saw the marks made on it and said something to herself.

The old man she took him to looked up in surprise to see her entering with the exhausted wolf following her.

She showed him the chain.

"We've been expecting you, little brother," the man said to Silver. "We will raise you and one day you will fulfill your destiny."

They were very good to him, and life was comfortable and filled with new friends. But in a few months, he became impatient, as if life was going by him and nothing was happening. He felt he was failing to do what he had so much energy and longing to finish.

One night when this feeling was especially strong, he had a dream of a woman who walked on two legs in the manner of his new family. He heard her call to him so he approached her.

"My friend, I am Buffalo Woman. Long ago, I took the sacred pipe to the Lakota people. Through it, they learned to walk the earth in truth and with respect. Now it is time for us to take the pipe to the De'ne. They will recognize us. They have a legend that a woman and a wolf will bring them a holy pipe."

Silver awoke and went to the place where, in his dream, the woman had appeared. He waited.

Several days went by and some people from the village came to find out what had happened to their friend. They tried to urge him back. He would not go. So they respected him and left him there alone. At the end of the fourth day, he saw a woman approaching.

She was as beautiful in the two-legged's way as he was among the wolf family. As he walked toward her, she spoke.

"My friend, you are here. That is good. The world is ready for us now. The world is ready for peace. This is the sacred pipe that will teach respect, for respect is the peace."

Silver looked long at the object in her hands. It had on it symbols of two-leggeds, four-leggeds, leafed, and feathered ones. His mind flashed back to his father's words. "There is something you must carry. Something important."

As he looked at the woman for a moment, her eyes seemed to be those of his father's—with the pride and knowledge that he would prove worthy.

"Can they talk to us?" he had asked his father.

"Some can—those who walk in spirit," was the answer.

The thoughts of Silver and Buffalo Woman, in a few minutes, became one. They walked with great dignity into the village.

But suddenly the woman stopped and looked for a long time at the form of the being before her, the young wolf she had known for so long, yet had just met.

"Our message of respect for all of life, dear Silver, is not really our message. It is what we learned from four lifetimes.

"You walked with me when I was a black woman, a white woman, an Asian woman, and now a Native American woman.

"The greatness of all these people is in us and the lessons of respect we learned from each."

Something in what she was saying and the way their spirits sent messages to each other answered a question. Silver began to understand why the people in all the villages seemed to know him and he fit in so well and understood so much.

Now they were entering the cabin of the old man whose name had once been placed on a she-wolf's chain. When they appeared, the old holy man smiled, raised his right arm to where the sun would sit at mid-afternoon and spoke.

"We will prepare for your appearance before our council this day. Welcome, we knew Silver would bring you to us."

As I finished the story, then, in 1985, and again while writing this chapter as I near 65 years, in 2005, I hope it will help fulfill the mission and go places I will never be able to go.

The story has been available to my students to read, through my Job Corps teaching years, and last year, an "at-risk" student wrote this about the story.

"I really thought that this 'furry tale' was a cute and moving story. It told me that no matter who leaves you, that you have love. Just keep the faith and they will be with you always.

"I think Silver was very brave for taking off on his own. What I think was going through his mind at that time was 'I have to do this for my family.'

"If I had found a man that has known my mother, it would make me feel very comforted to know that someone else had seen what kind of person she was. I bet Silver was pleased and interested in this man."

After the story, I asked the students to write one question and answer about the story. Hers was "What were the villages Silver had to pass through? Blacks, whites, Asian Americans, Native Americans."

Wolf of Yukon had told me of how the northern Athabascans would nearly starve to keep from killing off the caribou during the lean cycles. He said they would eat mice rather than deplete the herds.

One of our conversations was about his Chiricahua relative and hero, Cochise. He said that after Cochise was forced to surrender, General George Crook was dispatched to the Dakotas to do the same to Sitting Bull and his people. Wolf said his people believed that the spirit of Cochise and the spirit of Sitting Bull joined. He mentioned Dee Brown's *Bury My Heart at Wounded Knee*. In reading it, it is interesting to note that Cochise died in 1874, and by 1876 General Crook was in the thick of the Lakota fight for their Black Hills with Sitting Bull in a leadership role.

On a lighter note, Wolf told of joining the Marines as a pilot and wanting to visit his remote Yukon home. So he was dropped by parachute. His father saw that and wanted to do it. Wolf tried to dissuade him. When the 70 year old insisted, Wolf told him how to guide the chute over the lake for a soft landing. Then he took him up. But the wind shifted and the elderly man bumped hard on land and was not happy.

Wolf told of taking his mother to Whitehorse, Yukon, to shop for the first time. When he returned to the airport, the entire runway was covered with groceries she had bought, in awe of all the new things.

He told of being shot in Vietnam and his German Shepherd battle comrade dragging him several miles to base. He picked splinters out for a long time, he said. He also had to learn to walk on a metal leg.

These conversations took place in the early 1970s, I was visiting Wolf at the prison. During the over a year I visited him, I wrote the following poems, discovered in storage on my birthday, June 12, 2007.

On the Road to You

Trees were green along the trail
It was warm to feel the air
In August, September, too
On the road to you.

Then the leaves were gold and red
The river felt this and it bled
It was fall, it was the view
On the road to you.

Now the leaves are gone, and white
Fills the limbs and every sight
On the road I feel the joy
Forever of girl on her way to boy.

Waiting For Mail

Roses are red, violets are blue
Give me a stroke from a letter from you
Syrup is sticky, also is sap
Do I detect a credibility gap?
"You'll get a letter. I mailed it today."
And strangely it comes an invisible way.
I talk to the postman, I moan and I wail
I accuse him of posting invisible mail.
If that's what he calls his pony express
He'd do a lot better with a mule or an ass
But still I believe and I check that square box
I don't need no theorem, just write of your sox.
                    Blue Eyes (His parents had named me)

I do have a binder of letters he wrote me. In one, he drew on his MIT physics degree to talk about the question of God and afterlife. Do they exist? He said matter is neither created nor destroyed. It just changes from matter to energy and back and forth. So when we die we become energy, but we can, in that energy form, work with matter, or become matter again, as needed.

Chapter Five

As Fools Crow's prophecies for me began to play out, and in September, February, April, and August, I met the four trees, men loving their people and leading me into the spirit world, I began to question why I had been chosen to receive this knowledge and pass it on.

But yet I didn't really wonder. One raised in the beauty of harmony with all of creation would not know the power of it as much as one raised in separation from that harmony. Or be willing to give her life to let people use her as a ladder to climb up the holy mountain, one hard step by one hard step.

Let us go to the concept of birth and motherhood. From a loving spirit world is born a child who at birth expects to be placed in loving hands. If that mother is mentally ill and hits and shuts the child in a room where her cries cannot be heard, all of life becomes fearful.

Fear of separation from love births all other fears, fear of abandonment, fear of worthlessness, fear of a world where darkness, not light rules.

As I grew up, I was told society must punish the "criminals" such as my mother who had abused me. I looked at my mother and knew she did not need punishment, she needed love. She needed an environment of harmony.

As I grew up, I was told some churches say God judges and condemns. I looked at my mother and me and knew our fears would be one day outshone by a loving God, not a vengeful God.

At this point, at 28, I went to Kate and Frank Fools Crow. And I learned from traveling and camping with them what many people have said about Fools Crow. If you asked him the difference between secular and spiritual life, he would say all of life is spiritual. Everything is soaked in spirit, and actions come from that understanding.

So here had come a fear-ridden woman to live with a couple so based in a loving Great Spirit that every thought and action was flowing from that Spirit!!

Soon, I had begun to soak up that spirit enough to help cure my birth mother. Now, it would be time to soak up enough to help cure my earth mother. Red Horse's Fire wrote in his *Lord of the Dawn* book a beautiful passage about how father sky sends his love to earth mother. I share it in the passage below.

The second tree on the stone had taken me to Sitting Bull's grave, the location before he was moved to an inaccessible place. I lay in the grave, crying, because the prophesied trees given to me were always taken from me. The second tree was told "This woman with the dust of Sitting Bull matted to her tears has a special task."

Sometime later, I wrote the following to Sitting Bull.

Dear Sitting Bull,
Your eyes penetrate, for what do you look?
Perhaps I should kneel, for I read in a book
Of your people, your spirit, your knowledge of truth
Before this I stand, from a race in its youth.

Long ago I lay in your grave
Crying, because no person they gave
Was meant to stay with me, I wanted to die
Obedience put me there, there let me lie.

Then faith raised me up and now I can't kneel
I can't be unworthy, for you cannot feel
Love for a weakling. As I had lain there
Did you ask why this woman was chosen to bear
The job of teaching all you had been?
To help us see clearly, I must write this, then.

What I'm not, my chief, I must grow to be
This crooked stem must become a tree
From this cluttered mind there must glow a star
My jumbled words must grow straight, go far.

What I bring to you is a will to live
For every ill one you want to give
The power that lies in your people's ways
That protects them from any white people craze.

There Are Four Trees On Your Stone

The power that makes you buffalo chief
Who plants himself between herd and thief
Defying alone any threat to the herd
Protected from bullets at your Maker's word

My chief, you've a gaze that penetrates
The face and the paper that dumbly states
Man owns the earth who gave birth to the man
Can man own the Power that created the plan?

Can man live by himself, use the trees, use the lives
That belong to all ages, belong to all tribes
Killing today to make himself rich
Making the earth a burial ditch?

Your eyes seeing deeply, your hand cannot grasp
The pen and approve what your mind will not grasp.

So little I know still, my chief, of you,
Our cultures so different can we ever break through
The impatience in your heart with the orphan in mine
So unready still for a family divine.

When you penetrate, for what do you look?
Perhaps I should kneel, for my vision once took
Me away on a journey with people so pure
I stood with my hang-ups, how unworthy we were.

But faith raised me up and now I can't kneel
Why was I chosen? No one can feel
As can one born in darkness surrounded by hate
The rays of the sun, the love of a mate.

No blossom as rare on tree that was groomed
As on tree bent and knarled and thought to be doomed
Sun reflects not a brightly from eyes use to light
As from eyes that kept hoping through eternal night.

The innocent, living among just their kind
Know not the test of a bombarded mind
From birth hearing sickness, bitterness, pain

Learning the fear of even God's rain.
Fear of the thunder, animals, sin
Even a baby tears its mother's skin.

Out of this hatred for life to begin
Where can we find the stillness, the blend
Of man and creator in which we can rest
And have faith to love and build a warm nest.

And know there is blessing in life-giving rain
Hear his love in thunder, find no animal plain,
Each an expression of a loving earth
Eternally grateful for a new day to birth

All that awakened in her when she reached
Her mountains to sky, and sky never preached
To her of some strange sin that does not make sense
In a world that loves openly as the Maker intends.

But rather, that sky warmed her with sun
Caressed her with wind, her heart had been won
He began to grow heavy with passion for her
He thundered, she felt her own body stir.

He gave then, completely, his spirit, his rain,
And all grew alert, her body became
So full of new life, it had to reach high
As she had toward her husband, the sky.

Can all of this poetry; come—I must ask it—
From one who once thought life ends in a casket
And begins when a terrible animal, man,
Forces a woman with some selfish plan.

Why comes a poem from one raised like this?
Is the truth as pretty to ones raised in bliss?
Is it so important to them it be writ
To heal every orphan hungry to sit

On the lap of earth mother who welcomed his birth
When no two parents told him his worth

*And longs for his father to shine down some proof
To his mother and him there is warmth and a roof.*

*I read your words, my chief, your truth
And know it will strengthen the people's rebirth
And from the high mountain I've had to grasp for
They'll see all the truths of our past lives, and more.*

Chapter Six

The last time my son and I saw Frank and Kate Fools Crow is an exciting tale of Olympic gold medals, saving the Black Hills, coming of the Dawn for Native America, and saying goodbye to two of the most powerful role models/teachers in my life.

The year was 1987. The third Lakota (Sioux) tree on the stone had written *Quetzalcoatl, Lord of the Dawn,* in 1971, and finished it in Oaxaca (wa ha' ca), Mexico. There we meditated under the world's oldest living tree as had Quetzalcoatl. The book prophesied that in 1987, the nine 52-year-cycles of hell, based on the Aztec calendar, would end and the dawn would break.

The year, 1987, dawned for us in Eagle River, Alaska. Needing to be with our adopted Lakota people for the coming of the Dawn, we flew south stopping in California to visit family members.

While there, I found a magazine article written by Billy Mills, the Lakota who won a gold medal in the Olympics in 1964. In the article, the Pine Ridge Reservation hero wrote of a trip to see Fools Crow. He asked the holy man he revered if he, Billy, had forsaken his people by being a Christian, and working in California. Fools Crow had told him there is one Creator, it doesn't matter what you call him. And Billy Mills was to follow his dream, wherever it took him.

We were not far from Billy's town in California, so I purchased an old car that had to have water put in the radiator every few miles and away we went. Dinner at an open air restaurant with Billy and his wife, Pat, was a wonderful experience. At that dinner we heard of the movie of his life, *Running Brave,* and that he had set up the Billy Mills Indian Youth Leadership Program.

From the movie seen years later, we learned that what had kept him going during the grueling Olympic preparation and the run itself was the knowledge of what it would mean to other American Indian youth if he would win.

This was another example of how living for the people gave the Native Americans that extra courage and energy needed to become the powerful people they are. As we watched the movie, we felt his triumph over slurs he faced at Haskell Indian Institute, the University of Kansas, Lawrence, and even at the Olympics. Top runners received running shoes from a local store in Tokyo, but since he was a long shot, they refused him as he stood at the checkout counter with the shoes he had picked out. He had to borrow shoes to run in.

He not only won, but he broke the American record and set a new Olympic mark of 28 minutes, 24.4 seconds for the 10,000 meter race.

Mills told me at that dinner in California, that when we got to South Dakota, I could use him as a reference to Editor Tim Giaga of the "Lakota Times" for a job. That did help, and soon I was working as a reporter in the small Rosebud Reservation town of Martin, South Dakota. My son spent his days with full-blood Lakota Bill and Annie Apple and their children. For years after, when we were making a decision about materialism or sharing, we would ask "What would Bill and Annie do?" The answer always was generosity.

Then came the trip back from Martin, S.D, to Kyle, S.D., that summer of 1987. The paper had assigned me to cover a meeting at Oglala College during which traditional people were trying to save the sacred Black Hills from being invaded by Honeywell's ammunition division. We got to the meeting before anyone else, and noticed there were rows of seats for the Lakota, and facing them, a row of seats for the Honeywell Corp. executives. I told my son that this was not right. Lakota council circles put everyone at equal status. So we rearranged the chairs in a circle before anyone got there.

Descendents of Black Elk and other honored traditional people (some I recognized from traveling with Fools Crow) confronted the executives with great power that day. When one lady warned Honeywell representatives that it was dangerous to take on the sacred powers of the Lakota, I followed her up by explaining that to realize the depth of her threat they must understand the very meaning of the word Lakota means friend or ally. The natural way is peace, harmony, and friendship, in their heritage. For her to become this angry, they need to understand that her ancestor, Black Elk, received his powerful vision for peace and unity in those Black Hills. I explained that many Lakota are very hungry, but have refused millions of dollars in government settlements for the Black

Hills. The thought of an ammunition plant and testing on grounds so sacred a people in poverty have turned down millions for them is unthinkable. There were many powerful speakers that day and they did not need a white reporter speaking for them. But something in me got very overpowering and I could not sit and say nothing.

When we went to Fools Crows' ranch near the college, we knew Kate would not be there. We had visited her earlier at a nursing home in Martin, where we had a tearful meal and gave her our love.

A visit with Fools Crow, that day, found him at 95 or 96, still strong, active, and excited about a visit to the original Sacred Calf Pipe brought by the Buffalo Calf Woman centuries before,

He described his feelings the first time he was left alone with the Sacred Calf Pipe in Mailer's *Fools Crow*. Early in that book, he says the following.

"No ceremonial item is more important and vital to my people than the sacred pipe. It is not enough to call it a peace pipe. It is much more . . . Every Sioux pipe has its origin in the first pipe brought to my people by the holy Calf Pipe Woman, who is also called White Buffalo Calf Maiden. Since that time the pipe has been the central item in all our Sioux ceremonies and in our life way . . .

"Ever since it was first given, our Sacred Calf Pipe, which is wrapped in a cloth bundle, has been kept by a succession of custodians . . . It is presently kept in a small wooden building at Green Grass, on the Cheyenne River Reservation in South Dakota. The Keeper is Orval Looking Horse. He is a handsome young (this is in the 1970s when that book was written) Lakota man who lives according to our traditional ways and speaks little English . . . .

"In the old days, some Indian tribes had a special tribal ceremonial pipe that was only smoked when it was necessary to make a truce between enemies. Sometimes a pipe like this was placed on the ground between two enemy groups as a pledge of peace during trade talks . . ."

On an earlier visit of mine, in the 1970s, Fools Crow had drawn for me a picture of the original Sacred Pipe. On it were symbols from the two-leggeds, four-leggeds, winged ones, leafed ones (stem) and the stone from the earth. All these, the bringer of the pipe had said, were to be revered as holy.

At the age of 65, as I end this chapter in 2005, I hold the sacred pipe Fools Crow gave me 37 years ago. I pray to the west, where the sun goes down, teaching us to trust through the darkness that there will be a dawn; to the north, from where the north wind comes to test us and make us strong; to the east where the sun comes up giving us knowledge; to the south, from where the warm winds come and make all living things grow; and last, to father sky and mother earth, the parents of all orphans whose birth parents are gone, and parents to all who need their warmth, light, food, and loving place to walk. I ask all these powers to help me describe the great power of that sacred pipe as taught to me.

The smoke from the pipe goes into the air and is carried throughout the world. Our words and thoughts of respect and reverence for all of life go into the air and are carried throughout the world. And there is the peace. The greatest military in the world cannot kill all of its enemies. As today, the military kills some, and more pop up. But respect and reverence for each and every living thing can spread until there are no more enemies

Sacred Pipe given to the author by Fools Crow. Bag with beaded tree bearing the four colors (races) made by author.

Epilogue

Don't cry for me, my Lakota, your winyan would never leave you
I had to wander, to find my vision, I kept my promise, I have a plan now
Once there were great ones who walked lovingly on the earth
The lives they led, the blood they shed, was that the people would live
The tree would bloom once more. Oh, let my people live.

Many years went by, they walked once more. My life touched their lives,
Their lives touched mine. We saw the dawn, and the tree becoming green
Just as the sun returned, and the people still live.
Don't cry for earth, my Lakota, you know you kept the vision. You passed the test now, the dawn is breaking.
You'll bring the dawn and the people still live.

As I was finalizing this book in 2013, I was reading Henry Thoreau's *Walden* along with my son, and Wayne Dyer's book on living the wisdom of the Tao along with my sister. (*Change Your Thought, Change Your Life.*)

The books both fit Fools Crow in recommending seeing deeply into the spiritual in every moment. Thoreau, in his cabin by a pond near Concord, Mass., lived with the birds. They were not in his yard, because he had no yard, he was part of the woods. Dyer quoted Rumi, "Every tree and plant in the meadow seemed to be dancing, those which average eyes could see as fixed and still."

On Bear Butte, this is the reality.

And both authors felt like the Lakota Red Cloud that the man-made things were not necessarily bad, but to look for the spirit use of them. When Red Cloud saw the teletype, he said it was only as good as the words that came over it.

Perhaps the cultures came together because those who had been told to have dominion over and created technology, needed to meet those who had learned to live in harmony with and to make spirit use of the technology. And perhaps it was time to hear the Asians who were told to allow things to happen in their own time, not hurry them. And surely it was time to learn from the black people who overcame not just for themselves, but because we are all better off when we respect each other.

Credits

Material used in book *There Are Four Trees On Your Stone*

Photo of Red Horse's Fire is from *The Praying Flute*, copyright by author Tony Shearer, published by Naturegraph Publishers, Inc., Happy Camp, California, 1987. Used with permission.

Photo of Eagle Man is from *Eagle Vision, Return of the Hoop*, copyright by author Ed McGaa, published by Four Directions Publishing, Minneapolis, Minnesota, 1998. Used with permission.

Photos of the El Tule Tree in El Tule, Oaxaca, Mexico, are from *Lord of the Dawn, Quetzalcoatl*, copyright by author Tony Shearer, published by Naturegraph Publishers, Inc. Happy Camp, California, 1971. Used with permission.

Photo of the book cover of *Night Flying Woman*, is of that book, copyrighted by the publisher, Minnesota Historical Society, 1983.

Quotes by Fools Crow, not in conversations with Jean Leonard, are reprinted from *Fools Crow*, by Thomas E. Mails, by permission of the University of Nebraska Press, copyright 1979 by Thomas E. Mails.

All other photos, including the cover, are by the author, Jean Leonard.

Edwards Brothers Malloy
Oxnard, CA USA
March 8, 2016